A treasure for you, O dear child
so you may know that Allaah
truly rose above His Throne.

Where is Allaah?

Author: Umm Faruq Mariam
Illustrator: Faruq ibn Saja
Editor: Umm Asiyah Ashanta Ambush
Reviewed by: Hassan Somali | Anwar Wright

Website: tarbiyahoutsidethebox.com
Email: info@tarbiyahoutsidethebox.com

ISBN: 9781513660400

Please note, the children depicted in this story are of kindergarten level (ages 5-6 years), hence the mixed gendered classroom.

Dear Parents,

Developing your child's love for Islaam begins early. We would like to help you along the way, in shaa Allaah. Coming upon authentic Islaamic children's books that captivate a child's interest, instills good morals, and teaches correct creed is akin to gold! With this as our aim, we've categorized our publications into four levels to help you choose from our titles based on your child's abilities.

Level 1 books introduce children to tawheed and Islaam at a very basic level using simple terminology.

Level 2 books explain the foundations of Islaam to young learners. Children at this stage are inquisitive and curious about their existence. These books are intended to address topics relevant to their growth and tarbiyah.

Level 3 books explore Islaamic concepts in more detail. Texts in this level take an in-depth look at topics in the religion, fostering a love of, and acquaintance with, Islaamic knowledge.

Level 4 books and materials are study aids to accompany trusted published books. Materials in this level are designed to help the youth interact with scholarly text.

Visit ***publication.tarbiyahoutsidethebox.com*** for information on our current and, in shaa Allaah, future publications, as well as ways you can foster a love of reading in your child!

Jazakum Allaahu khayran!
Tarbiyah Outside the Box

None is able to describe the true nature of His attributes. His affair cannot be encompassed and comprehended by the thinkers. He is above the glorified 'Arsh with His Essence and He is everywhere with His knowledge.

-Abu Muhammad 'Abdullah ibn Abi Zayd al-Qayrawani (d. 386 H)

ٱلرَّحْمَـٰنُ عَلَى ٱلْعَرْشِ ٱسْتَوَىٰ

The Most Beneficent [Allaah] Istiwaa [rose over] the [Mighty] Throne [in a manner that suits His Majesty].

Taahaa 20:5

The children in Sister Amina's class love so many things about their school day.

They love painting with all the colors of the rainbow, counting with their favorite wooden blocks, recess in the fresh outdoors...

.... and of course, center time.

But best of all, they love....

....story time!

Their bright, cheery classroom is always bustling with activity, but they all settle down when Sister Amina calls them to the story rug.

It always begins a bit like this.

"Claaaaas!", Sister Amina says with a cheerful smile.

"Yesss!" The children respond excitedly, as they hurry to the cozy green rug.

"Class, class!"

"Yes, yes!"

"My sweet class!"

"My sweet yes!"

The children find their spots and gather around their teacher.

"Do you know what time it is?"

"Yeaah! It's story time!"

"That's right! Sit close, dear children, and listen well."

The children sit patiently waiting for Sister Amina to begin.

Prophet Muhammad ﷺ was sent by Allaah to teach us our religion. He taught us many, many things.

He taught us about the prayer, fasting in *Ramadhaan*, paying *Zakah*, and *Hajj*.

The Prophet ﷺ also taught us other important matters about the Attributes of Allaah which Allaah mentions in the Qur'aan. From these Attributes is that Allaah is high above everything.

Long, long ago, during the Prophet's ﷺ time many people of Arabia, including some of the *Sahaabah*, had servants and helpers under their care. The servants were responsible for helping with daily chores, taking care of the land, and looking after the animals.

In one famous *hadith*, we learn of a *Sahaabi* named Mu'aawiyah ibn al-Hakam as-Sulami رضي الله عنه.

Under Mu'aawiyah's رضي الله عنه care was a girl responsible for watching and taking care of his sheep.

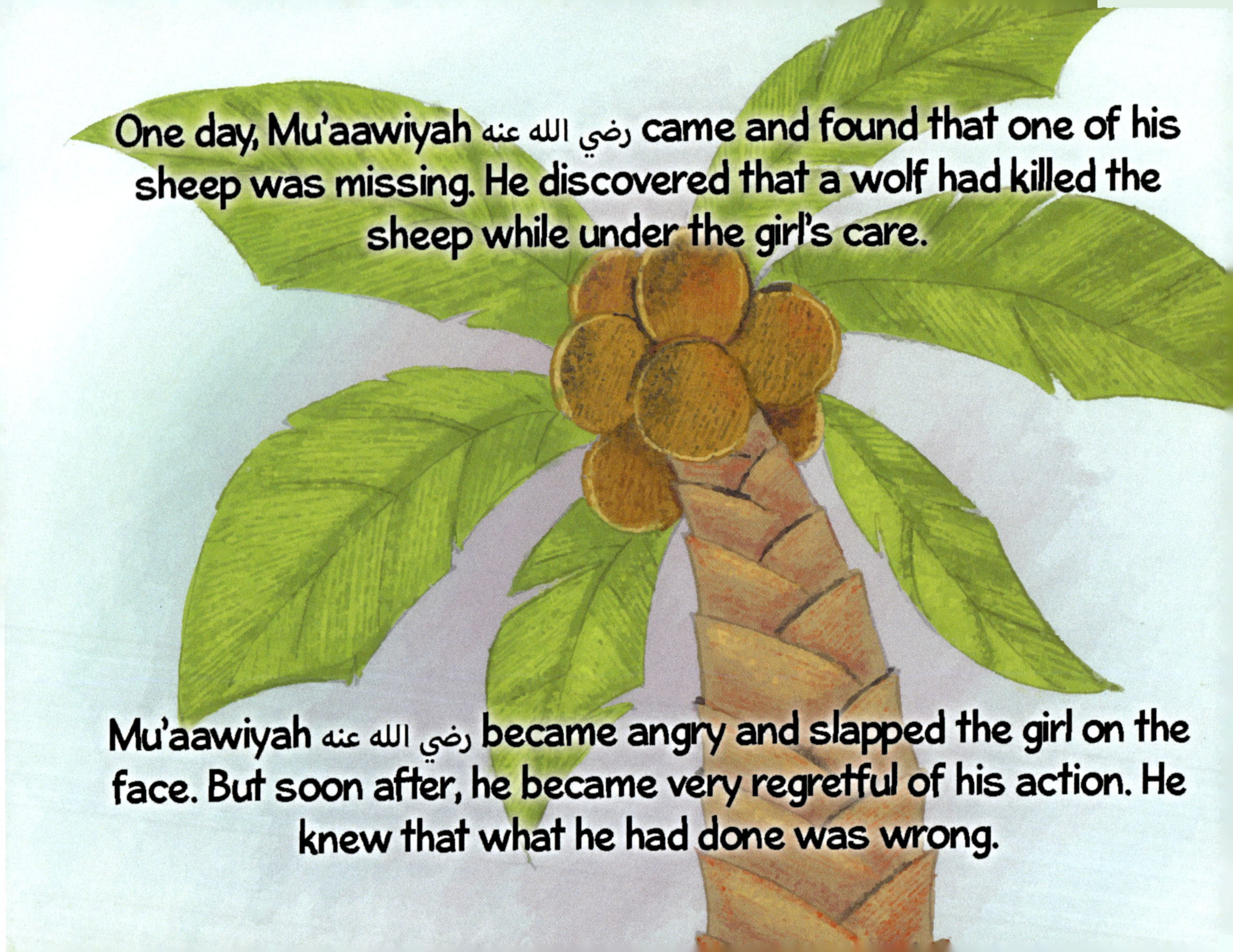

One day, Mu'aawiyah رضي الله عنه came and found that one of his sheep was missing. He discovered that a wolf had killed the sheep while under the girl's care.

Mu'aawiyah رضي الله عنه became angry and slapped the girl on the face. But soon after, he became very regretful of his action. He knew that what he had done was wrong.

Seeking guidance, he decided to go to the Prophet ﷺ for he
wanted to set the girl free in order to gain Allaah's forgiveness.

Mu'aawiyah رضي الله عنه said, "Oh Messenger of Allaah, should I not set her free?"

The Prophet ﷺ replied, "Bring her to me."

So, Mu'aawiyah رضي الله عنه went in search of the girl and brought her to the Messenger of Allaah ﷺ.

He ﷺ said to her, "*Ayn Allaah* — where is Allaah?"

She answered, "*Fees-sammaa* — above the heavens."

He ﷺ then asked her another question, "Who am I?"

She replied confidently, "You are the Messenger of Allaah."

After answering both questions correctly, the Messenger of Allaah ﷺ said to Mu'aawiyah رضي الله عنه,
"Free her, for verily she is a believer."

Know, O children, that Allaah is above the heavens, above His *'Arsh*-Throne. He is separate from His creation and His creation is separate from Him.

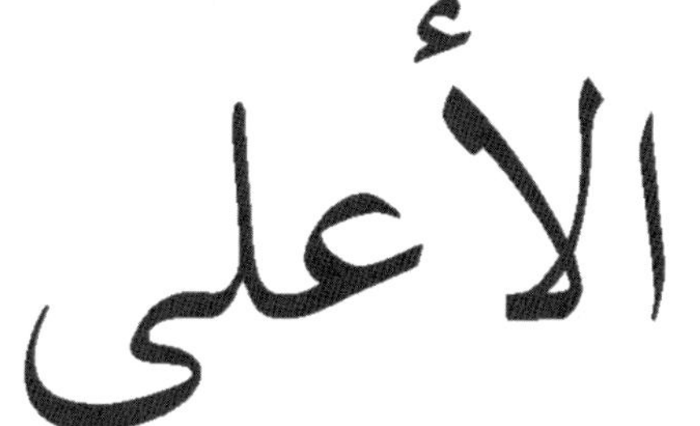

He is *al-'Alaa* — The Most High.

He is *al-'Alee* — The Lofty.

He is *al-Muta'aalee* — The Most High.

Beaming with joy, Sister Amina looks around the room at all of the children's beautiful smiling faces.

"Classity, classity!"

Excitedly, the children all respond, "Yessity, yessity!"

"Settle down, settle down."

"Who has a question for Ms. Amina?"

"Pick me, pick me!" A curly-haired boy squeals from the back of the room.

"Yes, Abdur-Rahman?"

"Ms. Amina, what if someone asks how is Allaah above His Throne? What do we have to tell them?"

Children, we believe in Allaah's eternal Attribute of *al-'Uluww* - Highness. This means Allaah has always and will always be described with highness above His creation. This never ever changes, as Allaah says in His Noble Book:

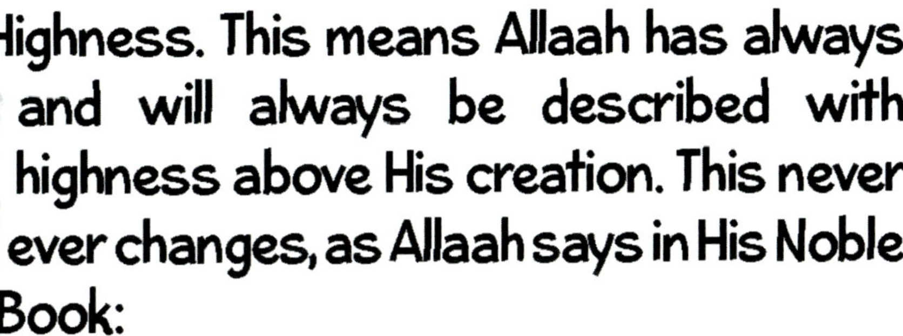

Glorify the name of your Lord, the Most High [87:1]

Indeed, Allaah has ever been Most High, Most Great. [4:34]

And He is the Most High, the Most Great. [2:255]

Know, O dear children, that it is not permissible for us to ask "how" or "why" when we talk about Allaah's Names and Attributes. Allaah is above His creation and above His Throne in a manner befitting His Majesty without asking "how".

In fact, there was once a man who asked about *al-Istiwaa* - Rising. He asked a scholar named Imaam Maalik رحمه آلله to tell him how Allaah rose over His Throne, and so Imaam Maalik رحمه آلله replied:

Al-Istiwaa ma'loom
Allaah's Istiwaa is known to us

wal kayf majhul
and the how is not known to us

wal-imaanu bihee wajib
and we must believe in it

wa sooalu 'anhu bidah.
and not ask about its specific details because doing so is a new thing that none of the *Sahaabah* ever did.

Children, we believe in Allaah's Attribute of *al-Istiwaa* - Rising. In the Qur'aan, Allaah tells us that He Rose over the *'Arsh*. He did so in a manner that befits His Majesty and only He knows the wisdom of His actions.

So boys and girls, we do not search out "how" Allaah Rose over the Throne, and it is not allowed for us to ask "why" He Rose over the Throne. We believe in it just as Prophet Muhammad ﷺ and his Companions did. They did not ask for details and neither do we.

"Does everyone understand?"

"Yesssss!"

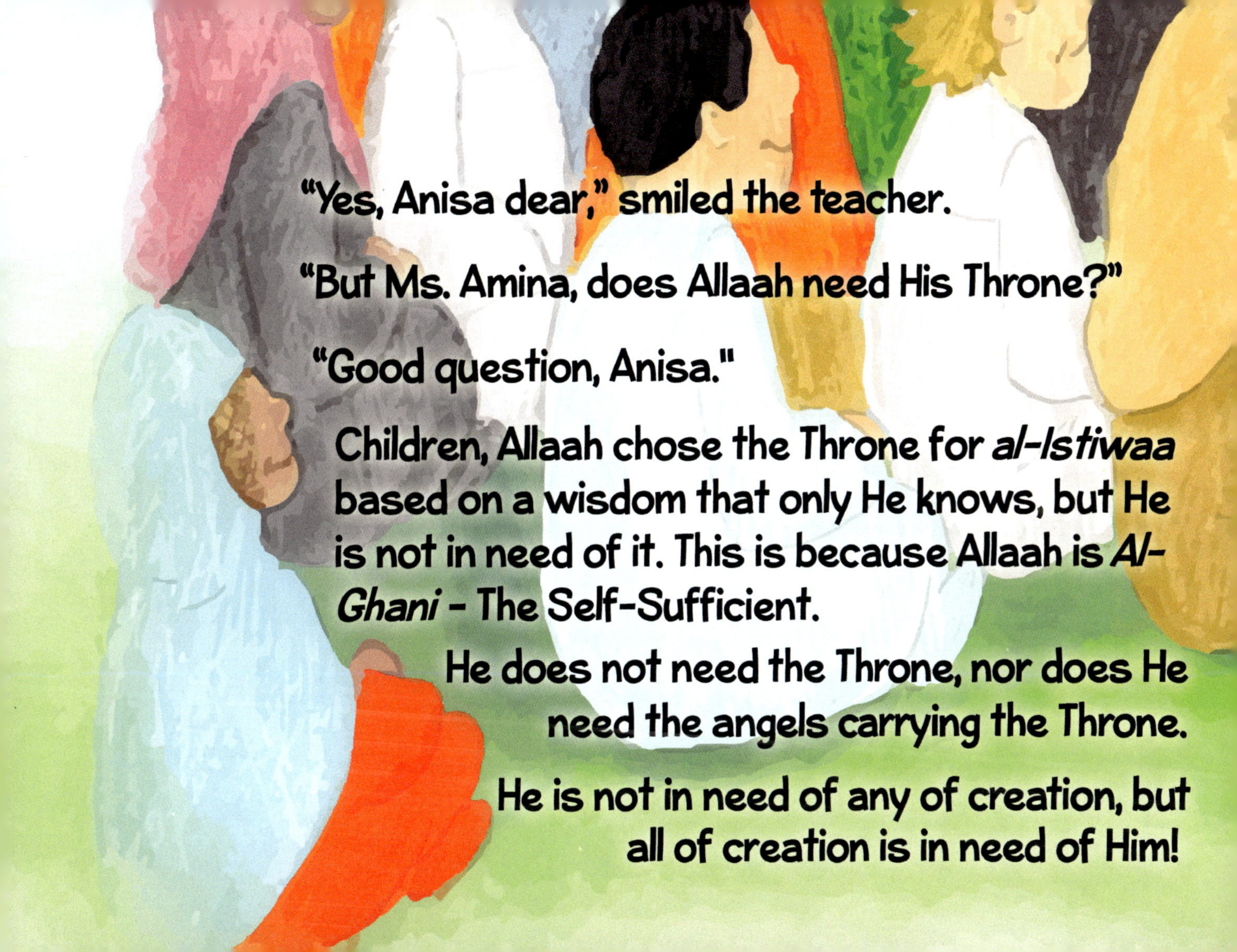

"Yes, Anisa dear," smiled the teacher.

"But Ms. Amina, does Allaah need His Throne?"

"Good question, Anisa."

Children, Allaah chose the Throne for *al-Istiwaa* based on a wisdom that only He knows, but He is not in need of it. This is because Allaah is *Al-Ghani* - The Self-Sufficient.

He does not need the Throne, nor does He need the angels carrying the Throne.

He is not in need of any of creation, but all of creation is in need of Him!

"Ms. Amina, Ms. Amina," Layla anxiously waits for her turn.
"May I ask a question too?"
"Yes, of course."

"My mom said Allaah is high above all of creation and that He knows everything we do. But Ms. Amina, how do we know soooo much about Allaah?"

"Well, Layla," the teacher happily responds,

"We know Allaah through His Names and Attributes that He mentioned in the Qur'aan and also through that which Prophet Muhammad ﷺ informed us about His Lord in the Sunnah!"

"Raise your hand if you understand."

"Meeeee!", they all cheer holding their hands high in the air.

"Does anyone else have a question?"

"Noooo!", the children reply in unison.

O dear children, whenever you are asked, "*Ayn Allaah* — where is Allaah?" Make sure to answer correctly and say:

"*fees-sammaa* — above the heavens" just as the servant girl did.

"She believed in Allaah, and so do we. We believe in the Messenger, and so did she!"

"*Ayn Allaah?*"

"*Fees-samaa!*"

"Yaaaaay", the children all cheer.

Appendix

Glossary of Terms

Word	Arabic	Definition
'Arsh	الْعَرْشُ	It is the greatest thing Allaah created.
Hadith	الْحَدِيثُ	It is a written record of the tradition of the Prophet ﷺ, - his actions, statements, and silent approval.
Hajj	الْحَجُّ	The fifth pillar of Islaam when Muslims make a pilgrimage to Makkah and fulfill specific rites.
Radi Allaahu anhu	رَضِيَ اللهُ عنه	A supplication said after the mention of a Companion, which means: may Allaah be pleased with him.
Raheemuhullaah	رَحِمَهُ ٱللَّهُ	May Allaah have mercy upon him.
Ramadhaan	رَمَضَانُ	The ninth month of the Islaamic calendar when Muslims fast daily, from dawn to dusk.
Sahaabah	الصحابة	Companions; plural for Sahaabi.

Sahaabi	الصَّحَابِيُّ	Companion; someone who met Prophet Muhammad ﷺ, believed in him and died as a Muslim.
Sal Allaahu 'alayhi wa salaam	ﷺ	A supplication said after the mention of the Prophet ﷺ, which means: may Allaah raise his rank and grant him peace.
Ta'teel	التَّعْطِيلُ	Denying the correct meaning of Allaah's Attributes that is established with proof.

Hadith of the Slave Girl

Mu'aawiyah ibn al-Hakam said: "I had a servant-girl who tended sheep for me in the di-rection of Uhud and Al-Jawaaniyaah and I came one day and found that a wolf had taken one of the sheep, and I am a man from the children of Aadam, I became angry as they do, and I hit her very hard. So I came to the Prophet sallallahu 'alayhi wa sallam and he made me aware of the seriousness of that, so I said: O Messenger of Allaah, shall I free her? He said: "Bring her." So I brought her and he said to her: "Where is Allaah?" She said: 'Above the sky.' He said: "Who am I?" She said: 'You are Allaah's Messenger.' He said: "Free her for she is a Believer.

Reported by Imam Muslim, Abu Dawood, and others

Reply of Imaam Maalik to the One Who Asked About Al-Istiwaa

It was narrated by Yahya ibn Yahya at-Tamimi and Ja'far Ibn 'Abd-Allaah and a group of them said:

"We were with Maalik when a man came and asked him: 'O Abu `Abd Allaah! "The Most Beneficent (Allaah) Istiwaa (Rose Over) the (Mighty) Throne (in a manner that suits His Majesty) (Ta-Ha 20:5). How did He Istiwaa (Rise Over)?"

Malik lowered his head and remained thus until he was completely soaked in sweat. Then he said:

"The Istiwaa (Allaah's Rising Over His Throne) is ma'qool (known); the "how" is majhool (inconceivable); belief in it is wajib (obligatory); asking about it is bid'ah (an innovation); and I fear that you are not anything but an innovator." Then he commanded that the man be removed."

Shaykh Al-Albaanee (rahimahullaah) declared this to be saheeh. Mukhthasar al-'Uluw of Dhahabee, Checked by Shaykh Naasir rahimahullaah, page 141

Deviated Sects Who Did not Affirm Allaah's Loftiness

Jahmiyyah

The Jahmiyyah are a deviant group who follow Jahm Ibn Safwan, who derived his beliefs from Greek philosophers, Sabeans, and the misguided Jews and Christians. They make *ta'teel* (denial) of Allaah's Names and Attributes, including the '*Uluww* of Allaah. They reject actions for Allaah and say there is no deity above the Throne. Likewise, they falsely claim that Allaah does not have speech and that the Qur 'aan is created.

Mu'tazilah

The Mu'tazilah are a misguided group who split from the Jahmiyyah. They pretend to affirm the Names of Allaah, while rejecting actions for Allaah and denying His Attributes, including Allaah's highness above the creation. They avoid affirming Attributes for Allaah by describing Him in negatives. They, too, make the false claim that the Qur'aan is created.

Ashaa 'irah

The Ashaa'irah are an innovated group who split from the Mu'tazilah. They ascribe themselves to Abu al-Hasan al-Asha'aree (may Allaah have mercy upon him) who used to be a Mu'tazli before Allaah guided him to the Sunnah. In reality, they follow the methodology of the Kullabiyyah (followers of 'Abdullaah ibn Sa'id ibn Kullab) and affirm the Names of Allaah, but deny all of Allaah's Attributes except for seven: Knowledge, Power, Will, Life, Hearing, Sight and Speech. They also reject the belief that Allaah has chosen actions. As relates to Allaah's 'Uluww (highness), they oppose the Jahmiyyah and Mu'tazilah and affirm it.

Quraanic Verses About Al-Istiwaa

إِنَّ رَبَّكُمُ ٱللَّهُ ٱلَّذِى خَلَقَ ٱلسَّمَـٰوَٰتِ وَٱلْأَرْضَ فِى سِتَّةِ أَيَّامٍ ثُمَّ ٱسْتَوَىٰ عَلَى ٱلْعَرْشِ

Indeed, your Lord is Allah, who created the heavens and earth in six days and then established Himself above the Throne.

A'raf 7:54

أَمْ أَمِنتُم مَّن فِى ٱلسَّمَآءِ أَن يُرْسِلَ عَلَيْكُمْ حَاصِبًا ۖ فَسَتَعْلَمُونَ كَيْفَ نَذِيرِ ١

Or do you feel secure that He who is above the heaven will not send against you a fierce whirlwind of stones? Then shall you know how (severe) was My warning.

Al-Mulk 67:17-18

وَهُوَ ٱللَّهُ فِى ٱلسَّمَـٰوَٰتِ وَفِى ٱلْأَرْضِ ۖ يَعْلَمُ سِرَّكُمْ وَجَهْرَكُمْ وَيَعْلَمُ مَا تَكْسِبُونَ

And He is Allah, [the only deity] in the heavens and the earth. He knows your secret and what you make public, and He knows that which you earn.

An'am 6:3

بَل رَّفَعَهُ ٱللَّهُ إِلَيۡهِۚ وَكَانَ ٱللَّهُ عَزِيزًا حَكِيمًا

Rather, Allah raised him to Himself. And ever is Allah Exalted in Might and Wise.

An-Nisa 4:158

يَخَافُونَ رَبَّهُم مِّن فَوۡقِهِمۡ وَيَفۡعَلُونَ مَا يُؤۡمَرُونَ۩

They fear their Lord above them, and they do what they are commanded.

Nahl 16:50

ٱللَّهُ لَآ إِلَٰهَ إِلَّا هُوَ ٱلۡحَيُّ ٱلۡقَيُّومُۚ لَا تَأۡخُذُهُۥ سِنَةٞ وَلَا نَوۡمٞۚ لَّهُۥ مَا فِي ٱلسَّمَٰوَٰتِ وَمَا فِي ٱلۡأَرۡضِۗ مَن ذَا ٱلَّذِي يَشۡفَعُ عِندَهُۥٓ إِلَّا بِإِذۡنِهِۦۚ يَعۡلَمُ مَا بَيۡنَ أَيۡدِيهِمۡ وَمَا خَلۡفَهُمۡۖ وَلَا يُحِيطُونَ بِشَيۡءٖ مِّنۡ عِلۡمِهِۦٓ إِلَّا بِمَا شَآءَۚ وَسِعَ كُرۡسِيُّهُ ٱلسَّمَٰوَٰتِ وَٱلۡأَرۡضَۖ وَلَا يَـُٔودُهُۥ حِفۡظُهُمَاۚ وَهُوَ ٱلۡعَلِيُّ ٱلۡعَظِيمُ

Allah - there is no deity [worthy of worship] except Him, the Ever-Living, the Sustainer of [all] existence. Neither drowsiness overtakes Him nor sleep. To Him belongs whatever is in the heavens and whatever is on the earth. Who is it that can intercede with Him except by His permission? He knows what is [presently] before them and what will be after them, and they encompass not a thing of His knowledge except for what He wills. His Kursi extends over the heavens and the earth, and their preservation tires Him not. And He is the Most High, the Most Great.

Baqarah 2:255

مَن كَانَ يُرِيدُ ٱلْعِزَّةَ فَلِلَّهِ ٱلْعِزَّةُ جَمِيعًا ۚ إِلَيْهِ يَصْعَدُ ٱلْكَلِمُ ٱلطَّيِّبُ وَٱلْعَمَلُ ٱلصَّـٰلِحُ يَرْفَعُهُۥ ۚ وَٱلَّذِينَ يَمْكُرُونَ ٱلسَّيِّـَٔاتِ لَهُمْ عَذَابٌ شَدِيدٌ ۖ وَمَكْرُ أُو۟لَـٰٓئِكَ هُوَ يَبُورُ

Whoever desires honor [through power] - then to Allah belongs all honor. To Him ascends good speech, and righteous work raises it. But they who plot evil deeds will have a severe punishment, and the plotting of those - it will perish.

Fatir 35:10

وَهُوَ ٱلْقَاهِرُ فَوْقَ عِبَادِهِۦ ۚ وَهُوَ ٱلْحَكِيمُ ٱلْخَبِيرُ

And He is the Invincible Subduer, above His servants (whom He dominates from every angle), and He is the all-Wise, well-Acquainted (with all things).

An'am: 18

تَعْرُجُ ٱلْمَلَـٰٓئِكَةُ وَٱلرُّوحُ إِلَيْهِ فِى يَوْمٍ كَانَ مِقْدَارُهُۥ خَمْسِينَ أَلْفَ سَنَةٍ

The angels and the Spirit will ascend to Him during a Day the extent of which is fifty thousand years.

Ma'arij 70:4

About Tarbiyah Outside the Box

Tarbiyah Outside the Box is an Islaamic parenting blog dedicated to the cultivation of the Muslim youth upon the understanding of the Companions and the early generations of Muslims who followed them. Our resources are designed for Muslim parents, guardians, teachers, and anyone in the position of the tarbiyah (education and cultivation) of Muslim children.

Through engaging, creative, and child-friendly resources, we hope to help ease some of the challenges Muslim parents face in finding quality, authentically-sourced Islaamic materials. Additionally, we hope to support a generation of Muslim children who will develop a strong sense of emaan, adherence to the Sunnah, and unapolegitcally bear their Muslim identity.

وَمَا تَوْفِيقِيٓ إِلَّا بِٱللَّهِ ۚ عَلَيْهِ تَوَكَّلْتُ وَإِلَيْهِ أُنِيبُ

And my success is not but through Allah. Upon him I have relied, and to Him I return.

Hud 11:88

Connect With Us!

	For Parents & Home Educators	For Classroom Teachers
Website	tarbiyahoutsidethebox.com	teachersoutsidethebox.com
Twitter	@tarbiyahbox	@muslimeducator
Instagram	@tarbiyahoutsidethebox	@teachersoutsidethebox
Facebook	fb.com/tarbiyahoutsidethebox	fb.com/teachersoutsidethebox
YouTube	youtube.com/TarbiyahOutsidetheBox	

Made in the USA
Middletown, DE
19 July 2020